APPROVED

Getting a New View of You

By Beth Jones

Harrison House

Approved: Getting a New View of You
ISBN 13: 978-160683-643-9
Copyright © 2010, 2014 by Beth Jones
www.jeffandbethjones.org

Published by Harrison House Publishers
www.harrisonhouse.com

CONTENTS

CHAPTER 1
Rejection 101

Been rejected lately? Dissed, disrespected, dismissed, disregarded, disapproved and dejected? There is not much we crave more than being approved, accepted and respected. However, we are often looking for approval in all the wrong places.

How I Learned This Lesson

Loserville. I was a senior in high school and no one asked me to the prom. I was so bummed out! I was devastated and felt like a major reject. Ever had a lump in your throat for weeks at a time? Several months before the big night, all my friends were talking about their dresses and where they were going to dinner. They buzzed with excitement while I sat quietly, not even wanting to acknowledge that I wasn't going. Rejected. Humiliated. Embarrassed. Seriously dissed. That's how I felt.

I really hadn't dated anyone since ninth grade. So, why was I surprised? Somehow, I just hoped that someone would ask me to the senior prom. During that time, a spirit of rejection began to take hold in my life. I felt so unwanted. So ugly. So unlovable.

My parents had been divorced from the time I was in sixth grade. Perhaps it was after my dad left that the seeds of rejection set in. (I was not aware of it at the time and I doubt anyone observing my life would have guessed how I felt.) On the outside, I was surrounded by a group of great girlfriends to hang with. Our group ran around with a group of boys and we all partied together most of our high school years. I was class president several times, played varsity basketball and enjoyed a fair degree of popularity in my school, but when it came to boyfriends—I felt like a reject! Not being asked to the prom took the cake. Now it was confirmed. I WAS a certified reject!

Before you pull out your Kleenex to wipe the big salties . . . let me tell you the end of this pitiful story. About four weeks before prom, I was at my dad's house during one of our weekend visits and he asked me about prom. I was very quiet and didn't say too much about it. He realized that I was devastated, so he did the most humiliating yet most wonderful thing!

Without my knowledge, he called one of his friends, who just happened to have an 18-year-old son, Kurt. My dad told Kurt about my dilemma and offered to pay him $100 if he would ask me to the prom. Is that mortifying or what? Is that the most pitiful thing you've ever heard?

It's a good thing I didn't know about it at the time, because this would have been my interpretation of the conversation: "Hello, Kurt? This is Jerry. I have a huge favor to ask. My loser daughter is such a reject no one has asked her to the prom, and I beg you, I'll give you a hundred bucks if you will please take her to the prom." Well, Kurt was a nice guy (and I'm sure the $100 bucks didn't hurt either!), so he asked me to prom. Since I didn't know about the payoff, I was thrilled to say yes! We went to prom and here's what I found out—prom isn't THAT big of a deal! It was okay, but not the highlight of my life. I didn't find out about the "prom bribe" until about five years after the fact, and I was absolutely mortified and absolutely thrilled that my dad would do such a thing!

As it turned out in my life, God used this prom experience, along with other times that I felt the pangs of rejection, to take me on a wonderful journey with Him in His Word. Now, I would like to take you along with me on this adventure so you too can enjoy a life free from rejection or inferiority!

What About You?

Ever been rejected? Overlooked? Perhaps you've even felt the same way I felt. Maybe it wasn't a prom that confirmed your reject status; maybe it was something that created larger scars on the inside of you. Maybe you've been abused and mistreated by people you thought you could trust. Maybe you've felt rejected by people because of your appearance, skin color, gender, handicap, or social or economic status. Perhaps you've felt disappointed by a job promotion you didn't get, or a broken engagement that broke your heart. Maybe you've felt rejected by your parents. A boyfriend? A girlfriend? A boss? A professor? A friend? Or not accepted because you're too tall? Too short? Too skinny? Too fat? You don't fit the mold? Maybe complete strangers have rejected you? Maybe it's your faith in Jesus Christ that's caused you to feel rejected?

If you're a parent, perhaps your children have rejected a relationship with you by talking back or making fun of your old-fashioned ways. If you're a student, maybe you've been bullied or put down at school because you wear the wrong clothes, hairstyle or shoes. In the adult world—at work or in the neighborhood—you can feel rejected when people talk behind your back or don't invite you to the company party. People can be mean and with the social media factor, people can say some of the most mean-spirited things online that they wouldn't have the courage to say to your face. All of these things hurt.

If you've ever been one of the last ones picked for a team; if you've ever asked someone out and heard the words "no"; if you've sat by the phone that never rang; if you've gotten a "Dear John/Dear Jane" letter; if anyone has ever hung up on you, not answered your e-mail, deliberately not "liked" your posts, ignored you with the silent treatment; read you the riot act—then you know how it feels to be the Mayor of Loserville. The list goes on . . . if you've ever received a "rejection" letter, been divorced, let go, fired, dumped, excluded or ostracized—you have felt rejected, dejected and dissed. It doesn't have to be dramatic, sometimes a string of small things leaves you feeling overlooked and invisible. Whatever it is, God wants to free you from a spirit of rejection.

Describe a time you felt rejected or dissed:

NUGGET: Sometimes you may feel alone, but you're not. Everyone has felt rejected—even the most secure, confident, together person you know! Somewhere, sometime in their lives they have felt the pain of being rejected and not accepted. Experts tell us that 90% of the population walks around with a low self-esteem and self-image. This tells us that there are a lot of people in our society who feel rejected in some way.

Perhaps you've noticed that sometimes those who act the hardest on the outside feel the most rejected on the inside. Often, people put up barriers to protect themselves from further rejection. They've learned that if they don't get close to people, they can protect themselves from further heartbreak and pain. In effect, they attract the very thing they fear. As they install walls of bitterness, anger, criticism, sarcasm and toughness, they give off an air of self-sufficiency, which pushes people further away, and the rejection cycle continues.

Drs. James and Connie Messina, Certified Clinical Mental Health Counselors and licensed counseling psychologists, describe the following attributes as characteristics of rejection or the fear of rejection:[1]

1. State of being of individuals who are over-dependent on the approval, recognition, or affirmation of others in order to feel good about themselves. In order to sustain personal feelings of adequacy, these individuals are constantly concerned with the reactions of others to them.

2. Irrational fear that others will not accept me for who I am, what I believe, and how I act.

3. Pervasive motivator for caution in my behavior and interactions with others.

4. State of mind that makes me incapable of doing or saying anything for fear of others' rejection, lack of acceptance, or disapproval.

5. Self-censoring attitude that inhibits creativity, productivity, and imagination in one's approach.

6. Driving force behind many people that keeps them from being authentic human beings. They are so driven by the need for acceptance of others that they lose their own identity in the process. They mimic the ways in which others act, dress, talk, think, believe, and function. They become the three-dimensional clones of the "role models" they so desperately need to emulate in order to gain acceptance.

7. Underlying process in the power of "peer pressure" that grabs hold and makes people act in stereotypic, "pop" culture, counter culture, punk, new wave, preppie, yuppie, and other styles. They crave recognition and acceptance from the reference group with whom they want to be identified.

8. Energy-robbing attitude that leads to self-immobilization, self-defeating, and self-destructive behavior. This attitude encourages ongoing irrational thinking and behavior, resulting in personal stagnation, regression, and depression.

9. Driving force of some people for all actions in their lives. It plays a part in their choices concerning their education, career direction, work behavior, achievement level, interpersonal and marital relationships, family and community life, and the ways in which they spend leisure time.

10. Act of giving to others more power than I give to myself over how I feel about myself. What the others say or feel about me is the determinant of how I feel about myself. I am completely at the mercy of others for how happy or sad I will be. My self-satisfaction and belief in myself is in their hands. Fear of rejection is the abdication of power and control over my own life.

Do any of these characteristics describe you? If so, which ones?

In what ways do you see that you've had symptoms of rejection or the fear of rejection?

Let's look at God's Word on this subject.

God Understands Rejection

1. Isaiah 53:3-11

    In this passage, underline any word or phrase that describes rejection, brokenness or hurt.

    > He was despised and rejected—a man of sorrows, acquaint-ed with deepest grief. We turned our backs on him and looked the other way. He was despised, and we did not care. Yet it was our weaknesses he carried; it was our sorrows that weighed him down. And we thought his troubles were a punishment from God, a punishment for his own sins! But he was pierced for our rebellion, crushed for our sins. He was beaten so we could be whole. He was whipped so we could be healed. All of us, like sheep, have strayed away. We have left God's paths to follow our own. Yet the LORD laid on him the sins of us all. He was oppressed and treated harshly, yet he never said a word.
    >
    > He was led like a lamb to the slaughter. And as a sheep is silent before the shearers, he did not open his mouth. Unjustly con-demned, he was led away. No one cared that he died without descendants, that his life was cut short in midstream. But he was struck down for the rebellion of my people. He had done no wrong and had never deceived anyone. But he was buried like a criminal; he was put in a rich man's grave. But it was the LORD's good plan to crush him and cause him grief. Yet when his life is made an offering for sin, he will have many descen-

dants. He will enjoy a long life, and the LORD's good plan will prosper in his hands. When he sees all that is accomplished by his anguish, he will be satisfied. And because of his experience, my righteous servant will make it possible for many to be counted righteous, for he will bear all their sins (NLT).

Jesus knows what it means to be rejected. He was despised and rejected! He totally understands what it feels like to be hurt, excluded, misunderstood, ignored and treated poorly. He was rejected by man and on the cross as He bore our sin, He was rejected by His Father. Do you know why Jesus experienced rejection? He was rejected as our substitute. He really didn't deserve to be rejected or despised, but He took upon Himself all that would make a person unacceptable before God, so we would not be rejected. He took what we really deserved!

It is the enemy's plan to create distance and separation between us and God. He wants us to feel inferior and unacceptable to God. The last thing the devil wants is for you to recognize and experience God's acceptance through Jesus Christ. This is the very reason Jesus came. Because of sin, we were separated from God—we were rejected. Sin would have kept us permanently separated from God, if Jesus had not taken our sins upon Himself and become our substitute. On the cross, He took the punishment we deserved. Jesus was rejected so that we could be accepted.

How did people treat Jesus?

Whose weaknesses and sorrows did He carry?

Why was He wounded and crushed?

Why was He beaten?

Why was He whipped?

Because of all that He experienced, what did He make possible?

He made it possible for you and me to be accepted—to be found righteous and acceptable in God's sight and among men.

Think about it. What would it mean to you if you were convinced that God accepted you?

2. Isaiah 61:1-3

Underline any phrase that describes healing, comfort and acceptance.

"The Spirit of the Lord GOD is upon Me, because the LORD has anointed Me to preach good tidings to the poor;

He has sent Me to heal the brokenhearted, to proclaim liberty to the captives, and the opening of the prison to those who are bound; to proclaim the acceptable year of the LORD, and the day of vengeance of our God; to comfort all who mourn, to console those who mourn in Zion, to give them beauty for ashes, the oil of joy for mourning, the garment of praise for the spirit of heaviness; that they may be called trees of righteousness,

The planting of the LORD, that He may be glorified" (NKJV).

Jesus came to heal the brokenhearted! The rejected. The hurting. Aren't you glad? He came to bring liberty to those who have felt captive in areas of their lives. He came to free us from spiritual, emotional, physical and mental bondages and prison walls that have kept us locked up!

What type of "year" did Jesus come to proclaim?

NUGGET: Notice that He came to preach the acceptable year! God wants you to know, by experience, the sense of acceptance and not rejection. God's acceptance means God's favor. And God's favor means God's acceptance!

What do we receive as a result of this "acceptable" year?

What does God want us to be called?

We'll look at the subject of righteousness in the next chapter.

God Loves and Accepts You

1. Isaiah 49:14-16

    Underline the words that describe God's love for you.

> *Yet Jerusalem says, "The LORD has deserted us; the LORD has forgotten us." Never! Can a mother forget her nursing child? Can she feel no love for the child she has borne? But even if that were possible, I would not forget you! See, I have written your name on the palms of my hands. Always in my mind is a picture of Jerusalem's walls in ruins (NLT).*

God promises that He won't desert, reject or forget you! He loves you like a mother loves her new baby!

Describe the love a new mother has for her nursing child.

Why is it that He will not forget us?

2. 1 Chronicles 4:9-10

Underline the four things that Jabez prayed for.

> *And Jabez was more honourable than his brethren: and his mother called his name Jabez, saying, Because I bare him with sorrow. And Jabez called on the God of Israel, saying, Oh that thou wouldest bless me indeed, and enlarge my coast, and that thine hand might be with me, and that thou wouldest keep me from evil, that it may not grieve me! And God granted him that which he requested (KJV).*

NUGGET: Perhaps you've read the book, **The Prayer of Jabez** and discovered this magnificent prayer! Jabez may have been acquainted with the sense of rejection or being dissed. After all, his mother named him "Jabez," which means "to grieve, sorrowful." Talk about feeling like an unwanted child! We don't know why his mother named him that. Perhaps she experienced great pain and sorrow giving birth. So now Jabez had to be reminded of that for the rest of his life. Perhaps she was a single mother who faced an unwanted pregnancy that caused her sorrow. We don't know what happened, but we do know that Jabez started his life with a sense of grief and sorrow. The Amplified Bible refers to Jabez' name as: "sorrow maker."

How would you like to be reminded of the pain, grief and sorrow your birth caused, every time someone called your name? Can you imagine? Today, it might be like being named, "Pain in the neck" or "Unwanted." That might make you feel just a little unacceptable and rejected! Maybe you can relate to Jabez. Perhaps your parents have told you that they didn't want you, or you've heard how much grief and pain you've caused others. Maybe you've been told that people wish you had never been born. It's painful to deal with those types of things, but God, through Jesus Christ, has provided healing and help for you. Did you notice what Jabez did—in spite of his label? He prayed! He asked God to do something that a reject doesn't deserve!

What four things did Jabez ask God to do for him?

What did God do?

God granted his request! Do you think God loved Jabez more than He loves you?

How about you? Are you ready to get some help? Are you ready to call on God and begin to experience the joy of being set free from any label or aroma of rejection? Make this your homework:

- Call on God.
- Ask God to bless you.
- Ask God to enlarge your influence for Him.
- Ask God to surround you with His hand of favor.
- Ask God to keep you wise and obedient in the place of protection from evil.

We've looked at Jabez and the sense of rejection he may have faced, now let's talk about why we sometimes feel rejected. Why do we sometimes feel rejected or fear rejection? Again, according to Drs. James and Connie Messina, those who feel rejection can be characterized by several factors, including:[2]

1. Lack healthy self-concepts, self-worth, or self-esteem because they were never fully affirmed in their families of origin.

2. Have had a traumatic experience of rejection, for example, in a divorce or separation that deeply scarred them.

3. Have lacked appropriate role models in life who accepted them for who they really were.

4. Have never been exposed to healthy ways of dealing with conflict or dis-agreement.

5. Lack the social skills to adapt to a reference group.

6. Have suffered from social isolation in their early lives.

7. Lack certain personal accomplishments, which they feel set them apart and which contribute to their lack of self-confidence.

8. Have a physical condition that they believe makes them unattractive to others.

9. Have been told all their life that they were "second best" or different.

10. Fear that others will not accept them for who they are, what they believe or how they act. Obviously, there are different degrees to which people are affected by a sense of rejection. It can range from minor hurt feelings to major debilitating fear. The good news is that God promises that He will never reject you.

God Will Never Leave or Reject You

1. Ephesians 1:3-6

   Underline the words, "chose" and "accepted in the Beloved."

   > *Blessed be the God and Father of our Lord Jesus Christ, who has blessed us with every spiritual blessing in the heavenly places in Christ, just as He chose us in Him before the foundation of the world, that we should be holy and without blame before Him in love, having predestined us to adoption as sons by Jesus Christ to Himself, according to the good pleasure of His will, to the praise of the glory of His grace, by which He made us accepted in the Beloved (NKJV).*

   You need to ponder the phrase, "He chose us . . ." Can you grasp that? God picked you! He wants you! He doesn't reject you, but rather He chose you! Let that soak in.Nugget: I remember going roller-skating at the local rink when I was in junior high. Every night, they would have the "Snowball Skate." This was the dreaded "somebody-please-pick-me" skate! All the girls would line up along the wall, and the boys would skate around and pick a girl to skate with during the Snowball Skate song. I always hoped someone would pick me, but I usually ended up skating off the rink by myself, feeling like a reject. Then I would stand on the sidelines and watch all the girls who got picked, skate with their dreamy boys. Well, guess what? God had a big Snowball Skate and He picked you! He saw you standing there, feeling inferior, insecure and lost—and He chose you!

What does it mean to be "in the Beloved"?

We are accepted! Through our faith in Him, God has placed us in Christ and we are completely accepted by God. Let that soak in. When you get a grip on the reality that God has accepted you completely through your union with Christ, the acceptance and rejection of others becomes less important to you.Nugget: God has not rejected you! He understands the reality of being rejected and brokenhearted so much that Jesus took our place and identified with our sense of inferiority, unworthiness and feelings of rejection, so we could experience the reality of being chosen and accepted by God. He came to heal the brokenhearted and to let us know that the time of being accepted is at hand. You and I are accepted in Christ!

2. John 6:37

Underline Jesus' promise to those who come to Him.

> *However, those the Father has given me will come to me, and I will never reject them (NLT).*

What will Jesus never do to you?

3. Hebrews 13:5-6

Underline the word "never."

> *"Never will I leave you; never will I forsake you." So we say with confidence, "The Lord is my helper; I will not be afraid. (NIV)*

What will God never do to you?

NUGGET: One of the ultimate forms of rejection is when someone you love leaves you. That is why divorce is so painful. To be rejected by someone you love is heartbreaking. As a baby Christian, I remember one night staying awake almost all night afraid that if I went to sleep, God would leave me. Sometime during that night as I read my Bible, I stumbled on Hebrews 13:5, *"I will never leave you nor forsake you" (NKJV).* As I read that verse of Scripture, God filled me with peace and the assurance that He would never leave me. I've often thought that my fear of God leaving me was connected to my parents' divorce and my dad leaving our family. It was such a comfort to know that God will never leave me, even if someone I love does. Be encouraged if you've faced the heartbreak of divorce or the pain of watching someone you love walk out of your life. God will never walk out on you!

I trust you have begun to grasp the reality that God understands the pain and hurt of being dissed, rejected and overlooked, but through our union with Jesus Christ He's provided the very thing we need—Acceptance!

Scriptures to Meditate On

The Spirit of the LORD is upon Me, because He has anointed Me
To preach the gospel to the poor;
He has sent Me to heal the brokenhearted,
To proclaim liberty to the captives
And recovery of sight to the blind,
To set at liberty those who are oppressed;
To proclaim the acceptable year of the Lord.
Luke 4:18-19, NKJV

Through the LORD's mercies we are not consumed,
Because His compassions fail not.
They are new every morning;
Great is Your faithfulness.
Lamentations 3:22-23, NKJV

Group Discussion

1. Describe a time in your life when your heart was broken by rejection or feeling overlooked. How did this experience affect you?

2. Describe the way you would feel emotionally, mentally and spiritually, if you knew and believed that God loved and accepted you unconditionally. What keeps you from believing this truth?

3. Describe the importance of being accepted by God and how that spills over into your other relationships. In other words, what kind of pressure is put on relationships when people are not convinced that God loves and accepts them?

---

[1] Used with permission from Dr. James Messina, www.coping.us

[2] Ibid.

CHAPTER 2
Blessed and Highly Favored

Who says you have to receive rejection? You can be the one who rejects rejection! What happens if you just choose to reject rejection? Author John Kador wrote a great rejecting rejection letter that goes like this:[1]

Dear ......,

Thank you for your letter rejecting my application for employment with your firm.

I have received rejections from an unusually large number of well qualified organizations. With such a varied and promising spectrum of rejections from which to select, it is impossible for me to consider them all. After careful deliberation, then, and because a number of firms have found me more unsuitable, I regret to inform you that I am unable to accept your rejection.

Despite your company's outstanding qualifications and previous experience in rejecting applicants, I find that your rejection does not meet with my requirements at this time. As a result, I will be starting employment with your firm on the first of the month.

Circumstances change and one can never know when new demands for rejection arise. Accordingly, I will keep your letter on file in case my requirements for rejection change.

Please do not regard this letter as a criticism of your qualifications in attempting to refuse me employment. I wish you the best of luck in rejecting future candidates.

Sincerely,
John Kador

Isn't that great? I believe God wants us to reject rejection by realizing who we are in Him. When we are confident in who He has made us, we can give rejection the boot. We are accepted in Him. Not only does He accept us, He pursues us!

A number of years ago, the popular worship leader Darlene Zschech wrote a song titled, *"Everything about You."* This song included this interesting line about her husband, *". . . you chased me, I caught you."* I love that line! That's exactly what Jesus has done for us! He chased us and we caught Him! He chased us down with His desire to forgive our sins, declare us righteous and to surround us with His favor. It's almost too good to be true; God first loved us and initiated a plan to catch us!

> **NUGGET:** I remember a time in my life when it occurred to me that Jesus chased me. He initiated. He chose me. He sought me. I was stunned! For some reason, I had thought that I was the one who sought Him and I was the one who accepted Him, but one day as I was singing and worshipping the Lord, He put this song in my heart and I titled it, "The Other Way Around."

The Other Way Around

I was the one, who thought that I found You,
but You were the One, and I was found by You.
I was the one, who thought that I sought Your face,
but You were the One, who sought me in the first place.
I was the one, who thought that I loved You,
but You were the One, that loved me first and true.
I was the one who thought I gave my life to You,
but You were the One, that gave Your life, My Redeemer, true.
All along, it was the other way around,
You sought me and chased me down.
You are the One, I now do see,
You loved me first and reached out to me.

I was the one, that You had in mind,
When You laid down Your life, on the cross divine.
You are the One that I worship and adore
And I am the one that longs for You more and more.

Let's look at how much God loves, favors and accepts us.

God Loves You

It sounds a bit cliché, doesn't it? Unfortunately, many people have not truly experienced God's love for themselves. Too many people see God as a big ogre or a mean judge who is ready to bop them when they mess up. The reality is that God loves you and has always loved you.

1. Jeremiah 31:3

    Underline the phrases "I have loved you" and "I have drawn you."

    The LORD appeared to us in the past, saying: "I have loved
    you with an everlasting love; I have drawn you with unfailing
    kindness" (NIV).

    How long has God loved you?

    What has He done with His loving-kindness?

    How has He done this in your life?

2. Isaiah 62:2-5,12

Underline the phrases that describe your old name and the phrases that describe your new name.

The nations will see your righteousness. World leaders will be blinded by your glory. And you will be given a new name by the LORD's own mouth. The LORD will hold you in his hand for all to see—a splendid crown in the hand of God. Never again will you be called "The Forsaken City" or "The Desolate Land." Your new name will be "The City of God's Delight" and "The Bride of God," for the LORD delights in you and will claim you as his bride. Your children will commit themselves to you, O Jerusalem, just as a young man commits himself to his bride. Then God will rejoice over you as a bridegroom rejoices over his bride.

They will be called "The Holy People" and "The People Redeemed by the LORD." And Jerusalem will be known as "The Desirable Place" and "The City No Longer Forsaken" (NLT).

Perhaps like Jabez (from our previous session), your name and identity was one of rejection and inferiority.

What did the Lord say He would do?

What would you not be called any longer?

What will you be called?

NUGGET: This prophetic verse tells us about the future of the great city of Jerusalem. It also tells us about our identity in Christ. Maybe it's time you began calling yourself what God calls you! In Jesus Christ, you are now called, "God's Delight, the Bride of God, Holy People, People Redeemed, Desirable, and No Longer Forsaken." Think about it—God's delight! Desirable! Wow!

God Chose You

1. John 15:16

Underline the words "choose" and "chose."

> You did not choose Me, but I chose you and appointed you that you should go and bear fruit, and that your fruit should remain, that whatever you ask the Father in My name He may give you (NKJV).

Did we choose Jesus?

Did Jesus choose us?

What does it mean to be chosen?

Why did He choose us?

2. 1 Corinthians 1:27-28

    Underline the word "chose."

    > Isn't it obvious that God deliberately chose men and women
    > that the culture overlooks and exploits and abuses, chose
    > these 'nobodies' to expose the hollow pretensions of the
    > 'somebodies'? (The Message).

    Who does God choose?

    What does this passage mean to you?

3. 2 Thessalonians 2:13

    Underline the words "God picked you."

    > Meanwhile, we've got our hands full continually thanking God
    > for you, our good friends — so loved by God! God picked you
    > out as his from the very start. Think of it: included in God's
    > original plan of salvation by the bond of faith in the living
    > truth (The Message).

    Why did God pick you?

4. 1 Peter 2:9-10

Underline the word "chosen."

> *But you are the ones chosen by God, chosen for the high call-*
> *ing of priestly work, chosen to be a holy people, God's instru-*
> *ments to do his work and speak out for him, to tell others of*
> *the night-and-day difference he made for you—from nothing*
> *to something, from rejected to accepted (The Message).*

Why did God choose you, according to this verse?

God brought us from "nothing to something" and from

"_____ to _____."

What does that mean to you?

God Made You Righteous

1. Romans 3:21-22

Underline the phrase "the righteousness of God."

> *But now the righteousness of God apart from the law is re-*
> *vealed, being witnessed by the Law and the Prophets, even*
> *the righteousness of God, through faith in Jesus Christ, to all*
> *and on all who believe (NKJV).*

What does this passage call righteousness?

This passage says that righteousness is a revelation. This righteousness is given to us completely separate and apart from our ability to keep the Law, the Ten Commandments, the rules and regulations in the Bible. Let's pray right now and ask God for the spirit of wisdom and revelation on this truth.

Dear Father God,
I ask You to give me the spirit of wisdom and revelation in obtaining the knowledge of righteousness. In Jesus' Name. Amen.

Righteousness: The basic definition of righteousness is "the way in which man may attain a state approved of God." It is also defined as, "the character or quality of being right or just"; it was formerly spelled "rightwiseness."[2]

NUGGET: I like the way one preacher defined righteousness: ***To be righteous in Christ is to be able to stand before God without any sense of unworthiness, guilt or inferiority as though sin has never existed.***

Are you convinced that God loves you? Because of His love for you and His acceptance of you in Jesus Christ, He has given you the great free gift of being righteous in His sight, of obtaining the righteousness of God. Think about this! One of the greatest revelations you will ever receive from the Word of God is the reality of righteousness.

Most people are sin-conscious; that is, they are primarily aware and conscious of their failings, their sins, their flaws and their mistakes, which results in a sense of inferiority, unworthiness, condemnation and rejection. God does not want His children to be sin-conscious, but rather He wants us to be righteousness-conscious. Too many Christians still see themselves as the unworthy worm they were before they accepted Jesus Christ and His forgiveness, and they have failed to see who they have become in Christ—brand new, forgiven and made righteous in His sight! The day you really understand righteousness—that God sees you in Christ as a person without any sense of inferiority as though you have never sinned—is a day of great freedom. That is a day of great joy. That is God's absolute will for you!

The righteousness of God is given to whom?

Is it for the select, perfect, super-Christians?

2. 2 Corinthians 5:21

Underline the phrase "the righteousness of God."

For He made Him who knew no sin to be sin for us, that we might become the righteousness of God in Him (NKJV).

Jesus was made sin (and thus rejected and despised) for whom?

Why did He do this?

In Him, what have we become?

How righteous is God?

Describe a person who knows that he is righteous in God's sight:

Can you believe this? Can you accept this reality? In God's sight, because you are in Christ, He sees you as righteous as He is! I hope you feel the guilt, condemnation, inferiority and rejection sliding off you!

3. Romans 5:17

Underline the phrase "the gift of righteousness."

> *How much more will those who receive God's abundant pro-vision of grace and of the gift of righteousness reign in life through the one man, Jesus Christ! (NIV).*

When we receive abundant grace and the gift of righteousness, what do we do in life?

NUGGET: What's the bottom line? God loves you! He chased you. He loved you first. He initiated it. When you receive His love by receiv-ing Jesus Christ, He immediately sees you in Christ—accepted, righteous and surrounded with His favor!

God Favors You

Do you have a favorite memory? A favorite friend? A favorite place to vacation? A favorite Scripture? Has anyone ever done you a great favor? Perhaps, it was something you didn't deserve or pay for but for whatever reason, someone decided to do you a favor that totally blessed your life.

You are God's favorite! All of His children are His favorites, and He is constantly doing favors for us. We are favored by God, simply because we are in His Son, Jesus Christ. Jesus paid the price and we got a deal we didn't deserve!

> **NUGGET: When God accepts us and gives us His righteousness, we are surrounded with His favor. God favors you. God's favor is the most wonderful thing—to have the God of the universe going to bat for you just because He loves you and has made you His righteousness is a great blessing! God's favor always has a purpose. When He favors you, it's because He has a divine, redemptive purpose in mind. Psalm 5:12**

In this passage, underline the word "favor."

> *For You, O LORD, will bless the righteous; with favor You will surround him as with a shield (NKJV).*

Are you righteous?

According to what we just studied, you are!

What do you base your righteousness on?

What does God promise the righteous?

How would you define "favor"?

Favor: This word is huge! It covers so much of God's goodness toward us. Favor means "a pleasure, a delight, a favor, goodwill, acceptance, a will."[3] When God surrounds you with favor, He surrounds you with acceptance. Consider that again—He surrounds you with favors. He surrounds you with pleasure and delight. God's favor gives you preferential treatment, open doors, opportunities, special benefits, promotions and goodness—just because His favor surrounds you like a shield. Do you believe it? Isn't that an awesome reality?

2. Proverbs 3:1-4

Underline the phrase "favor with both God and people."

> *My child, never forget the things I have taught you. Store my commands in your heart. If you do this, you will live many years, and your life will be satisfying. Never let loyalty and kindness leave you! Tie them around your neck as a reminder. Write them deep within your heart. Then you will find favor with both God and people, and you will earn a good reputation (NLT).*

Not only will God surround your life with His favor and acceptance, but He will also give you favor and acceptance in the eyes of people.

If we want favor with God and people, what should we focus on?

Who's Who

Here's a partial list of the Bible characters who received God's favor. Underline the name of each person/group that received favor and circle the type of favor they received, if it is mentioned.

> *But the LORD was with Joseph and showed him mercy, and He gave him favor in the sight of the keeper of the prison. Genesis 39:21, NKJV*

> *And I will give this people favor in the sight of the Egyptians; and it shall be, when you go, that you shall not go empty-handed. But every woman shall ask of her neighbor, namely, of her who dwells near her house, articles of silver, articles of gold, and clothing; and you shall put them on your sons and on your daughters. So you shall plunder the Egyptians. Exodus 3:21-22, NKJV*

> *And the LORD had given the people favor in the sight of the Egyptians, so that they granted them what they requested. Thus they plundered the Egyptians. Exodus 12:36, NKJV*

> *The king loved Esther more than all the other women, and she obtained grace and favor in his sight more than all the virgins; so he set the royal crown upon her head and made her queen instead of Vashti. Esther 2:17, NKJV*

> *Now God had brought Daniel into the favor and goodwill of the chief of the eunuchs. Daniel 1:9, NKJV*

> *Then the angel said to her, "Do not be afraid, Mary, for you have found favor with God." Luke 1:30, NKJV*

What did God's favor do for these people of God?

Hook up with God's favor like these believers did! God will grant you favor, not because you deserve it, but simply because He loves and accepts you as His child. Expect God's favor in every area of your life!

Scriptures to Meditate On

For the LORD God is a sun and shield; the LORD bestows favor and honor; no good thing does he withhold from those whose walk is blameless.

Psalm 84:11, NIV

For if by the one man's offense death reigned through the one, much more those who receive abundance of grace and of the gift of righteousness will reign in life through the One, Jesus Christ.

Romans 5:17, NKJV

Group Discussion

1. Describe a time you chased someone you loved, or a time someone who loved you chased you. How would you describe the idea of being chased?

2. Describe a time in your life when you lived under the weight of guilt, condemnation and a sense of inferiority or shame. In other words, how does it feel to be sin-conscious rather than righteousness-conscious? Have you discovered the freedom that comes from knowing you are completely righteous in Christ, as though sin never existed?

3. Describe a recent experience with God's favor in your life.

---

[1] Used by permission of the author, www.logicalnot.com

[2] *Thayer's Greek Lexicon*, Electronic Database, S.V. "righteousness."

[3] *Vine's Expository Dictionary of Biblical Words*, S.V. "favor."

CHAPTER 3
Edit Your Life

I hope by now you are convinced that God loves you and accepts you! Now the question is, how does this become practical and tangible in your life? How does this become more than just the greatest sounding theory you have ever heard? I've got good news for you. It's possible to experience God's acceptance in a tangible way. If you've struggled with feelings of rejection, you can be transformed. You can be a different person. You can feel different. You can think differently. You can literally be changed into another person.

I know this from experience. I am a different person today. I have experienced God's transforming power in my life. As I said, although on the outside no one would know it, internally I really struggled with a sense of rejection in my early Christian life until I began to get a hold of the truths in this study. God's Word transformed me.

If you've ever felt the heaviness of rejection or paralyzing hopelessness, or if you've ever felt unlovable and overlooked, you can experience the reality of feeling loveable.

Are you ready to edit your life? Are you willing to cooperate with God and watch His Word transform your life in this area?

You Can Be Transformed

1. Romans 12:2

    In this passage, underline the phrase "be transformed."

And do not be conformed to this world, but be transformed by the renewing of your mind, that you may prove what is that good and acceptable and perfect will of God (NKJV).

How would you describe being "transformed"?

Transformed: The Greek word for transformed is "metamorphoo." This means to transform (literally or figuratively, "metamorphose"). It's also translated as change, transfigure, transform.[1]

NUGGET: How transformed can you be? In various areas of your life, you can be as transformed as a caterpillar that turns into a butterfly. Did you study caterpillars and butterflies in grade school? You know the process of metamorphosis, right? A caterpillar spins a cocoon and the chrysalis is formed to facilitate the transformation of this caterpillar into a butterfly. This transformation is amazing. Now, let me ask you a question: have you ever confused a caterpillar with a butterfly? Of course not. Why? Because the process of transformation was so dramatic that the butterfly does not look anything like a caterpillar! The same thing is true when God's transforming power, His supernatural metamorphosis, goes to work in your life. You will be changed to such a degree that the new "accepted you" will not look anything at all like the old "rejected you"!

According to this passage, how are we transformed?

How would you define "renewing of the mind"?

Renewing of your mind literally means the renovation of your mind.[2]

God wants you to renovate your mind to His Word. He wants you to do a major "fixer upper" job on your thinking by replacing the old, negative, rejected thoughts with the new, true, accepted thoughts His Word is loaded with!

Have you ever been involved in a home renovation project? If so, describe it.

It takes work to renovate!

Are you ready to cooperate with God and His Word and put forth the effort it takes to renew or renovate your mind?

NUGGET: You need to get this! The primary way you experience transformation in any area of your life is by renovating, reprogramming and renewing your mind with God's Word! It's that simple and it's that powerful. As you begin to install new thoughts from God's Word into your mind regarding your acceptance in Christ, you will see the old "caterpillar you" transformed into a new "butterfly you." For example, when you read Ephesians 1, which tells you that you are "accepted in the beloved", you need to begin to renovate your mind with that very thought. To do this, you begin meditating on the reality that because you are a Christian in Christ, God accepts you completely. As you take time to ponder this thought, imagine what being accepted by God would look like, smell like and feel like. As you "paint" your mind with this Word from God, you will find yourself being transformed from the inside out. This new thought of acceptance will eventually demolish the old thought of rejection—your mind will be renovated and you will be transformed. The "rejected caterpillar" will be transformed into an "accepted butterfly."

2. 1 Samuel 10:6-11

Underline the phrase "you will be changed into a different person."

> *"The Spirit of the LORD will come powerfully upon you, and you will prophesy with them; and you will be changed into a different person. Once these signs are fulfilled, do whatever your hand finds to do, for God is with you.*
>
> *Go down ahead of me to Gilgal. I will surely come down to you to sacrifice burnt offerings and fellowship offerings, but you must wait seven days until I come to you and tell you what you are to do." As Saul turned to leave Samuel, God changed Saul's heart, and all these signs were fulfilled that day. When he and his servant arrived at Gibeah, a procession of prophets met him; the Spirit of God came powerfully upon him, and he joined in their prophesying. When all those who had formerly known him saw him prophesying with the prophets, they asked each other, "What is this that has happened to the son of Kish? Is Saul also among the prophets?" (NIV).*

What happened to Saul?

What was it that changed Saul?

What did Saul's old friends say?

What do you think was different about Saul?

NUGGET: We see the power of God changing Saul into a different person! Notice, it was God's Spirit coming upon Saul that changed him. We might say it this way today—when you allow God's presence through His Spirit and His Word to saturate your life, you will be changed! When the people who formerly knew Saul saw him, they couldn't believe it!

They wanted to know what had happened. This can be true of you, too! God will change you to such a degree that your old friends will scratch their heads and try to figure you out.

3. 2 Corinthians 3:18

    Underline the word "transfigured."

    > *And all of us, as with unveiled face, [because we] continued to behold [in the Word of God] as in a mirror the glory of the LORD, are constantly being transfigured into His very own image in ever increasing splendor and from one degree of glory to another; [for this comes] from the LORD [Who is] the Spirit (AMP).*

    If we continue to spend time renovating our minds to God's Word, the mirror, what will happen to us?

    What will we be transfigured or transformed into?

The good news is that you don't have to stay the way you are! You don't have to feel or be rejected!

God has shown us how to be transformed. We can experience a supernatural metamorphosis through the power of God's Word. Let the renovation project begin.

You can be transformed and you don't have to take rejection lying down. As you begin to see your value in God's eyes, you will be transformed into the confident person He sees you to be in Him.

NUGGET: There is no doubt that God's Word and His power can change our lives. At the same time, we also want to be honest with ourselves and God about why we are feeling rejected or overlooked. Is there a reason? Are we doing anything that would cause others to reject us? Are we being irritable? Difficult? Self-absorbed? Critical? Boring? Face it, no one wants to be around a "downer" or the person who is having a constant pity party. Are you making yourself enjoyable to be around? A pleasure to work with? Easy to talk to? We have a responsibility to be the type of person who exhibits godly qualities that people would enjoy being around.

Whatever the reason for our feelings of rejection through the power of God's Word, we can edit our lives. We can reinvent ourselves. We can "do over." It will require us to agree with God. We will have to renovate our minds with God's Word and this will take some effort on our part, but the results will be a dramatic transformation!

Scriptures to Meditate On

Now you're dressed in a new wardrobe. Every item of your new way of life is custom-made by the Creator, with his label on it. All the old fashions are now obsolete.

Colossians 3:10, The Message

So if the Son sets you free, you will be free indeed.

John 8:36, NIV

Group Discussion

1. Describe a home renovation project you have experienced—the blood, sweat and tears. How is this compared to the idea of renovating our minds?

2. Describe the changes others have seen in your life since Jesus became the Lord of your life. When your old friends saw you, what changes did they notice?

3. Describe the change and transformation that would be evident in a person who went from feeling rejected and overlooked to feeling accepted and confident. How would you describe their disposition, communication and general self-esteem?

---

[1] *Biblesoft's New Exhaustive Strong's Numbers and Concordance with Expanded Greek-Hebrew Dictionary.* S.V. "transformed."

[2] Ibid. S.V. "renewing."

CHAPTER 4
That's What I'm Talking About

When I was a young Christian in my mid-twenties, I was single and had a desire to meet Mr. Wonderful, get married and start a family, but the thoughts and feelings of rejection that went through my mind were sometimes paralyzing and the enemy used this to discourage me. At this time, I learned a life-changing truth.

As I meditated on God's Word regarding His acceptance and favor, I started to see myself the way God sees me—accepted, loveable and desirable. But I realized that it was not enough to just believe what the Word said about me; I needed to say what the Word said about me. Getting a grip on my lip was a huge turning point in my Christian life!

Like many sincere Christian girls, I had been praying for many years about the man whom I would marry. At the same time, I was growing in my walk with the Lord, Christian character and maturity. Yet, in my case, because the thoughts of rejection had been such a stronghold in my life, I had gotten into a bad habit of thinking, saying and feeling like no one would want me, which really caused me to struggle in my belief that anyone would. I knew I needed to renew my mind with God's thoughts and get my mouth speaking words that would turn the boat around. I realized I needed to take drastic measures to complete the process of supernatural transformation in this area of my life.

One day, I decided on a phrase that would become my new slogan. To some, this might sound ridiculous or even arrogant, but for me it was a life raft and it kept me afloat to the shores of acceptance and meeting Mr. Wonderful. My new phrase? *They all want me—bad!* Since inside myself, I felt like *No one will ever want me,* I knew that I needed to change that thought with a new one. So, it started as a tongue-in-cheek joke at first when I said, "They all want me—bad!" At that time, I didn't feel like anyone wanted me at all, but I knew I had to get my mouth in agreement with my desires and my faith. Of course, the enemy was right there with his negative thoughts, *Yeah right . . . they all want you . . . sure they do . . . who are you kidding? No one wants you, remember?* I just ignored those thoughts and continued to say to myself and my closest friends, "They all want me—bad!" It was a faith confession! As I continued to say this phrase, the most amazing thing happened—my thinking started to change and I started to feel that maybe someday, someone would want me after all. I continued to say, "They all want me—bad!" The more I said it, the more I started to believe it. And get this—the more I said it, the more I actually began to expect it!

Guess what? Within a short time, I met Jeff, my Mr. Wonderful who became my husband, and you'll never believe what he told me a few months after we were engaged. In one of our intimate moments, he said verbatim, "I want you bad!" Can you believe that? I can! God has given me "exceedingly more than I could ask or think" in Jeff. He is such a picture of God's love and acceptance in my life; it's almost unbelievable! But what makes it believable is that God promises us that we can be changed by the renewing of our minds, and as we'll see in this study, our words play a starring role in that transformation.

Your Words Are Shaping Your World

1. Proverbs 6:2

    Underline the phrase "snared by the words of your mouth."

    You are snared by the words of your mouth; you are taken by the words of your mouth (NKJV).

    What can the words of our mouth do to us?

Unfortunately, we are often being snared by our own words. When we say things like, "I am so ugly," "That just kills me," "He's driving me crazy," "I'm such a klutz," "No one will ever ask me out," and things like this, we are ensnaring ourselves with our words.

What negative words that are contrary to God's Word, are you saying about yourself and your life?

Are you willing to stop saying those negative words?

2. Hebrews 11:3

    Underline the phrase that tells us what framed the world.

    > *By faith we understand that the worlds were framed by the word of God, so that the things which are seen were not made of things which are visible (NKJV).*

    What framed the world?

    What were the visible things made with?

    NUGGET: Let's get the picture. God made the visible world with things that are not visible. He created the seen from the unseen. How did He do this? He framed (sounds like a renovation word, doesn't it?) the world with His words! He spoke words like, *Let there be light . . .* and there was light! He spoke words like, *Let us make man in our image . . .* and He made man! God's spoken Word created the reality of the world in which we now live. God's Word framed the world.

This principle of speaking God's Word is still in effect today. God's Word still has the power to frame our worlds. God created us in His image and likeness, so our words have the power to frame our world.

What type of world have you been framing (for yourself and others) with God's Word?

As we speak God's Word in our own lives, we will find that our world will become more congruent with His Word and His will. Let's look at the power of words.

3. Proverbs 18:21

Underline the phrase "the tongue has the power."

> *The tongue has the power of life and death, and those who love it will eat its fruit (NIV).*

Does our tongue have power?

Our tongue has what kind of power?

What fruit will we eat in our lives?

Can you see that your words will create life or death in your world? You eat the fruit of your words. If you don't like the fruit of your life, reflect for a moment and think about the words you have been saying.

4. James 3:3-6

Underline the words "bit," "rudder" and "spark."

> *When we put bits into the mouths of horses to make them obey us, we can turn the whole animal. Or take ships as an example. Although they are so large and are driven by strong winds, they are steered by a very small rudder wherever the pilot wants to go. Likewise, the tongue is a small part of the body, but it makes great boasts. Consider what a great forest is set on fire by a small spark. The tongue also is a fire, a world of evil among the parts of the body. It corrupts the whole body, sets the whole course of one's life on fire, and is itself set on fire by hell (NIV).*

This passage is talking about the power of the tongue in a negative way—it can corrupt the whole person. On the other hand, we see the power of the tongue to direct our lives.

What does the bit do in the horse's mouth?

Who determines what the bit does?

What does the rudder do on the ship?

Who determines what the rudder does?

What does a spark do?

Who determines the start of a spark?

Like the bit in the horse's mouth, the rudder on a ship, or like a spark, our tongue can direct the course of our lives as well!

What direction is your tongue taking you? What ports are your words taking you to? What fires are you starting with your mouth? Give some thought to the power of your words and make a decision to say things about your life that agree with God's Word.

Speak to Your Mountain

1. Mark 11:22-23

    Underline the words "says," "say," "whosoever" and "whatever."

    > *So Jesus answered and said to them, "Have faith in God. For assuredly, I say to you, whoever says to this mountain, 'Be removed and be cast into the sea,' and does not doubt in his heart, but believes that those things he says will be done, he will have whatever he says" (NKJV).*

NUGGET: Jesus revealed the power of our words in this passage. If you read Mark 11:13-24, you will see that the context of Jesus' lesson was the power of His speaking words to a fig tree. Jesus saw a fig tree that didn't have any fruit and He spoke words to that fig tree, telling it that it would not produce fruit again. He spoke loud enough for His disciples to hear. The next day when the disciples saw the fig tree that Jesus had cursed, withered up from its roots, they were amazed that the tree had obeyed His Words! Jesus responded to the disciples by saying, "Have faith in God!" In verses 23 and 24, Jesus then defines what faith in God looks like. A person with faith in God would speak to mountains. This person would believe the things he said. This person would have the things he said. Jesus made it so simple. Unfortunately, many Christians have stumbled over this idea of speaking words of faith by explaining it away and deleting it from their thinking and their theology.

According to this passage, is Jesus the only one who has the power or authority to speak words to things?

Who did Jesus authorize to speak to mountains?

According to verse 23, what can "whosoever" have?

Did Jesus say, "Speak to God about your mountain," or "Speak to the mountain directly"?

NUGGET: Many times people speak to God about their mountain, but Jesus told us to speak to the mountain by our faith in God!

Where are you not supposed to doubt?

When you speak words, what are you supposed to believe?

If you believe what you say, what will you have?

Ok, so what does this mean to us? It reminds us that our words have power to change our lives and circumstances! If you're facing mountains, you've got an answer. If the mountain of rejection is staring you in the face, get busy talking to that mountain. Start quoting God's Word over your life. Make your mouth and heart agree with God. He says you're accepted, so you better start saying, "I am accepted!"

2. Psalm 107:2

Underline the phrase "say so."

> *Let the redeemed of the LORD say so (NKJV).*

What are the redeemed supposed to do?

Have you been redeemed from rejection to acceptance?

Have you made it your practice to "say so"?

NUGGET: Your words have power! Where you are in life today is often a direct result of the words you spoke yesterday. Perhaps you will want to give some serious thought to changing your words and reframing your world with God's Word. Perhaps it's time to start talking to your mountain. Maybe it's time to be a better captain of the ship of your life. Get your mouth in agreement with God and His Word.

Scriptures to Meditate On

You are snared by the words of your mouth;
You are taken by the words of your mouth.

Proverbs 6:2, NKJV

A man will be satisfied with good by the fruit of his mouth.

Proverbs 12:14, NKJV

Group Discussion

1. What self-defeating words and phrases have kept you in bondage to feeings of rejection?

2. If you had to write a 60-second commercial for the "new" you, what would you say about your life? Write a commercial telling others why they should want you in their lives.

3. If you had to write a 60-second commercial for one of the people in your small group, what would you say about them? Write a commercial telling others why they would want this person in their lives.

CHAPTER 5
Sow Acceptance Seeds

I love spring! After a cold Michigan winter, it's great to see the daffodils and tulips spring up. I am constantly amazed at the miracle of how planting a bulb in the fall can result in a tulip in the spring. God's law of sowing and reaping, seedtime and harvest, is one of His best gifts to mankind! We do reap what we sow, and it's no less true in the area of acceptance.

One of the best ways to overcome your own weakness in this area is by simply sowing acceptance into the lives of others. Are you ready to plant seeds of love and acceptance? Let's turn the tables a bit and think about those around us. How can we help others experience acceptance? God created us to have relationships with others. Rich, intimate interpersonal relationships are one of God's most wonderful gifts. To reap these kinds of relationships, we must sow. How can we sow acceptance into the lives of others? It's easier than you might think.

Sow Interest

As Dale Carnegie once said, *"You can make more friends in two months by becoming interested in other people than you can in two years of trying to get other people interested in you.* I believe this is the most misunderstood secret to mutually enjoyable personal relationships. Think about it. When was the last time someone took note of the affairs, challenges, projects, dreams, events and dynamics of your world and asked you a meaningful question about your life? And then continued to show their interest by asking several good follow-up questions? If that has happened to you, you have a friend who is interested in your life.

I would bet that for most of you, this type of conversation has not taken place in a long time. In fact, it is likely that the most recent conversations you have had with family, friends or co-workers have revolved around them telling you stories about themselves. If you are a good friend, you asked them questions, showing your interest in their lives. My guess is that very few of you can honestly think of a person in your life who is consistent in asking you anything more than surface, cursory or courtesy questions. Why? Being interested in others and sowing acceptance in others goes against our selfish nature.

> **NUGGET: Most people want to feel noticed, liked, accepted, appreciated and approved of by the people who are important to them. We want people to want us. We have a need to know and be known. People want to disclose themselves to someone who is interested in them. All the human behavior and psychology experts will tell you that self-disclosure is a basic need of human beings. This creates a feeling of closeness between people.**

If we sow interest in others in an atmosphere of love and acceptance, we'll find a whole new level of rich relationships open up to us, replacing the fear of rejection.

I like what Christian author and founder of the Family Dynamics Institute, Joe Beam said in his article "Becoming Vulnerable": *"Removing all masks to let another see who we really are ('warts and all') means risking everything in that relationship. If the other person doesn't accept us when they encounter our undisguised selves, we feel absolute rejection. We likely won't continue the relationship, even if the other person wants to, because we know that he or she has seen the true us and been repulsed by the discovery. So how do we grow past that fear and decide to reveal our true selves? We do it in stages. We start by sharing facts that are non-threatening; facts that we feel won't be reacted to negatively. As we share those innocuous facts of our lives (e.g. "I was born in the USA,") we register every reaction of the person to whom we share. Any lack of interest or hint of displeasure on their part causes us to stop the process. We're certainly not going to reveal potentially threatening facts (e.g. "When I was a kid I was arrested,") if we note any dis-*

interest or rejection as we share innocuous facts. On the other hand, as we register interest and acceptance we tend to reveal more threatening facts. We can become so trusting of the seemingly unconditional acceptance of the other person that we tell him or her things about ourselves we've never told anyone."[1] When we sow interest in others, we help them to blossom in healthy ways, and we are bound to eventually reap the same. What does God's Word tell us about helping others overcome the hurt of rejection, dejection and being dissed by sowing acceptance and interest into their lives?

The Apostle Paul was good at sharing his heart and being vulnerable with others. Let's look at how he communicated the Gospel of Jesus Christ and his love, acceptance and care.

Cultivate Vulnerability in Yourself and Others

How vulnerable and transparent are you? Do you open up to and confide in the people in your life, or do you keep tight-lipped? Of course, there is a need for balance and learning how to navigate the tension between spilling our deepest feelings to total strangers and keeping an unhealthy distance from our friends and family. Self-disclosure, vulnerability and transparency are necessary for healthy relationships.

1. 2 Corinthians 6:11-13

    Underline the phrases "spoken freely," "opened wide our hearts" and "not withholding our affection."

    > *We have spoken freely to you, Corinthians, and opened wide our hearts to you. We are not withholding our affection from you, but you are withholding yours from us. As a fair exchange—I speak as to my children—open wide your hearts also (NIV).*

    I love how the Living Bible translates this passage: *Oh, my dear Corinthian friends! I have told you all my feelings; I love you with all my heart. Any coldness still between us is not because of any lack of love on my part* *but because your love is too small and does not reach out to me and draw me in. I am talking to you now as if you truly were my very own children. Open your hearts to us! Return our love!*What three things did Paul do to cultivate vulnerability?

Do you speak freely with others?

Do you open wide your heart to others?

Do you withhold your affection from others?

In what ways can you be more vulnerable in your relationships?

2. 1 Thessalonians 2:8

Underline the phrase "share with you."

> *Because we loved you so much, we were delighted to share with you not only the gospel of God but our lives as well (NIV).*

What two things should we share with others?

In your relationships, how do you share the Gospel and your own life?

How did Paul describe his feelings for these believers?

How to Be Genuinely Interested in Others

1. Philippians 2:19-22

    Underline the phrase "genuinely interested in your welfare and devoted to your interests."

    > *But I hope and trust in the Lord Jesus soon to send Timothy to you, so that I may also be encouraged and cheered by learning news of you. For I have no one like him [no one of so kindred a spirit] who will be so genuinely interested in your welfare and devoted to your interests. For the others all seek [to advance] their own interests, not those of Jesus Christ (the Messiah). But Timothy's tested worth you know, how as a son with his father he has toiled with me zealously in [serving and helping to advance] the good news (the Gospel) (AMP).*

    The Living Bible says it this way:

    > *There is no one like Timothy for having a real interest in you; everyone else seems to be worrying about his own plans and not those of Jesus Christ.*

    According to verse 20, what made Timothy stand out?

Are people like Timothy hard to find or commonplace?

What was Timothy truly interested in?

Was his interest "canned," "fake" or "shallow"?

What were others interested in?

In what ways could you be more like Timothy to the people in your life?

2. Philippians 2:4

   Underline the phrase "be interested in others."

   Don't just think about your own affairs, but be interested in others, too, and in what they are doing (TLB).

   What does this tell us concerning our interest in our own lives?

   What part of others' lives are we to be interested in?

3. John 16:5-6

Underline the phrase "none of you seems interested."

> *But now I am going away to the one who sent me; and none of you seems interested in the purpose of my going; none wonders why. Instead you are only filled with sorrow (TLB).*

What were the disciples not interested in?

What consumed their interest?

In what ways are we often consumed with our own issues, sorrows, and pity parties and not aware of the interests of those around us?

4. Zechariah 7:6

Underline the phrase "I'm interested in people."

> *And when you held feasts, was that for me? Hardly. You're interested in religion, I'm interested in people (The Message).*

What's the bottom line on what God is interested in?

NUGGET: When you show an interest in others, you are acting like God. You stand out because as the Apostle Paul said, there are not many people like Timothy who will naturally care for the interests of others. Let's be the kind of people who overcome our own sense of rejection by sowing acceptance and interest into the lives of others. As a result, we will reap our own harvest of acceptance, too!

If You Want to Have Friends, Be Friendly

1. Proverbs 18:24

Underline the phrase "be friendly."

> A man who has friends must himself be friendly, but there is a friend who sticks closer than a brother (NKJV).

If you want to have friends, what must you be?

How can you sow "friendliness" into the people in your life?

2. John 15:11-13

Underline the phrase that describes what friends do for each other.

> I have told you this so that my joy may be in you and that your joy may be complete. My command is this: Love each other as I have loved you. Greater love has no one than this: to lay down one's life for one's friends (NIV).

What does Jesus want to give us?

If we want to be filled with joy, how are we to love others?

How can we love our friends?

In what ways will you start sowing acceptance in their lives?

Scriptures to Meditate On

So this is my prayer: that your love will flourish and that you will not only love much but well. Learn to love appropriately. You need to use your head and test your feelings so that your love is sincere and intelligent, not sentimental gush. Live a lover's life, circumspect and exemplary, a life Jesus will be proud of: bountiful in fruits from the soul, making Jesus Christ attractive to all, getting everyone involved in the glory and praise of God.

Philippians 1:9-11, The Message

And may the Master pour on the love so it fills your lives and splashes over on everyone around you, just as it does from us to you.

1 Thessalonians 3:12, The Message

Group Discussion

1. Describe a time when someone sowed friendship and acceptance into your life.

2. Describe the challenges and strategies of sowing acceptance with others in these settings:

   - at a party
   - at school functions
   - at work
   - on social media
   - at church
   - in Bible studies
   - at reunions
   - when you are the new kid
   - in the neighborhood
   - with strangers
   - with family
   - when you're with adversaries

3. Describe, in general, a time you were vulnerable with a friend and how it knit your friendship together.

---

[1] Joel Beam, "Becoming Vulnerable," Gamily Dynamics Institute.com.www.familydynamics. net. Used by permission of the author.

CHAPTER 6
Just Like Jesus

Some rejection is inevitable! Jesus told us that. It's true that because of our union with Jesus Christ, we are totally accepted by God. At the same time, because of our alliance with Jesus Christ, we will experience rejection by others. People will mock, insult, and distance themselves from us because of our faith in Jesus Christ. Because of our identification with Him, we will face persecution and rejection. When this happens, Jesus told us to be happy about it. It's a confirmation that you're a Christian!

Have you ever experienced this? Have you had people look down at you because of your faith in Jesus Christ? Have you lost friends? Been ostracized? Ignored? Laughed at? Talked about? Made fun of? Rejected? Overlooked?

Anyone living the Christian life and carrying a solid Christian testimony is going to face persecution and rejection. The Bible tells us that all who live godly in Christ will suffer persecution. (2 Timothy 3:12). So, you can expect this type of rejection if you live a godly life. This is the "good" kind of rejection.

> NUGGET: Be sure you are being persecuted because of your good Christian testimony and not your flaky, obnoxious, self-righteous behavior. We all know Christians who have done more harm than good to the cause by their bizarre behavior. At the same time, very often, no matter how good your intentions are and how gracious your approach, you will be misunderstood, and people may reject you and your faith in Christ.

In some places around the world, people are experiencing severe persecution—torture and death—for their faith in Jesus Christ. In other places, the persecution is mild by comparison. In either case, Jesus had a lot to say about believers being rejected by the world.

If They Rejected Jesus, Guess What?

1. Matthew 5:10-12

    In this passage, underline the words "persecuted," "insult," "persecute" and "falsely say."

    > *Blessed are those who are persecuted because of righteous-*
    > *ness, for theirs is the kingdom of heaven. Blessed are you*
    > *when people insult you, persecute you and falsely say all*
    > *kinds of evil against you because of me. Rejoice and be glad,*
    > *because great is your reward in heaven, for in the same way*
    > *they persecuted the prophets who were before you (NIV).*

    How would you describe persecution?

    There is a definite sense of feeling rejected when people insult you because of your faith in Jesus Christ.

    What are we supposed to do when we are rejected because of our faith?

    What are we promised?

2. John 17:14-19

    Underline the phrase "the world has hated them."

I have given them your word and the world has hated them, for they are not of the world any more than I am of the world. My prayer is not that you take them out of the world but that you protect them from the evil one. They are not of the world, even as I am not of it. Sanctify them by the truth; your word is truth. As you sent me into the world, I have sent them into the world. For them I sanctify myself, that they too may be truly sanctified (NIV).

Why does the world hate the followers of Jesus?

3. John 15:19-22

Underline the phrases "the world hates you" and "if they persecuted me, they will persecute you."

If you belonged to the world, it would love you as its own. As it is, you do not belong to the world, but I have chosen you out of the world. That is why the world hates you. Remember what I told you: "A servant is not greater than his master." If they persecuted me, they will persecute you also. If they obeyed my teaching, they will obey yours also. They will treat you this way because of my name, for they do not know the one who sent me. If I had not come and spoken to them, they would not be guilty of sin; but now they have no excuse for their sin (NIV).

Why does the world hate those who follow Jesus?

Have you experienced this?

4. 1 Peter 4:4-5

    In this passage, underline the phrase "former friends."

    > *Of course, your former friends will be very surprised when you don't eagerly join them anymore in the wicked things they do, and they will laugh at you in contempt and scorn. But just remember that they must face the Judge of all, living and dead; they will be punished for the way they have lived (TLB).*

    What type of rejection/persecution will your former friends provide?

    Did you experience this type of rejection when you quit partying? Swearing? Watching or listening to ungodly music, movies, videos or television shows? Getting high? Going to the bars? Living together? If so, explain how you dealt with it.

    Who will everyone face?

5. 2 Timothy 3:12

    Underline the phrase "everyone who wants to live a godly life." Circle the phrase "will be persecuted."

    > *In fact, everyone who wants to live a godly life in Christ Jesus will be persecuted (NIV).*

    If you live a godly Christian life, what can you expect?

When you live your life based on God's Word, you are going to experience some persecution. When you make decisions that are not popular or that make others feel uneasy about their behavior, you will likely be rejected, despised, made fun of, excluded—persecuted! Make a decision that when this type of rejection comes your way, you will rejoice and praise the Lord anyway.

Remember, You're Never Alone

When you are rejected because of your faith, be encouraged to know that you really are not alone. Jesus promises to be with you always. It takes courage to be a Christian, to be a witness for Jesus, and to proclaim your faith to your family and friends. It hurts to be ostracized or overlooked because you are a Christian. Perhaps, you were overlooked for a job promotion, cut from the sports team, or laughed at and gossiped about in the dorm, office or neighborhood because of your faith in Jesus Christ. Often, the most painful form of rejection is when your own family persecutes you for your faith. In some cultures, when you become a Christian you are absolutely cut off and disowned by your family. Whether we are mocked, rejected and persecuted by our own family, close friends, co-workers or neighbors because of our Christian testimony and witness for Jesus Christ, we can find comfort knowing that God will never reject us. We are never alone!

1. Hebrews 13:5

   Underline the word "never."

   God has said, "Never will I leave you; never will I forsake you"
   (NIV).

   Though others may reject, leave, forsake and persecute you, will Jesus ever leave or forsake you?

2. Matthew 10:32-33

Underline the words "confesses/confess" and "deny/denies."

> *Therefore whoever confesses Me before men, him I will also*
> *confess before My Father who is in heaven. But whoever de-*
> *nies Me before men, him I will also deny before My Father*
> *who is in heaven (NKJV).*

If we acknowledge Jesus Christ, what will He do for us?

Remember, when you confess your faith in Jesus to others, Jesus is lis-
tening.

3. John 12:42-43

Underline the phrase "they loved the praise of men more than the praise of
God."

> *Nevertheless even among the rulers many believed in Him,*
> *but because of the Pharisees they did not confess Him, lest*
> *they should be put out of the synagogue; for they loved the*
> *praise of men more than the praise of God (NKJV).*

What did these people love?

Describe a time when you were faced with choosing either the "praise of
God" or the "praise of men."

4. Matthew 28:18-20

Underline the phrase "I am with you always."

> *He told his disciples, "I have been given all authority in heaven and earth. Therefore go and make disciples in all the nations, baptizing them into the name of the Father and of the Son and of the Holy Spirit, and then teach these new disciples to obey all the commands I have given you; and be sure of this—that I am with you always, even to the end of the world" (TLB).*

What did Jesus tell us to do?

What did He promise us?

Yes, as we preach the gospel we will face persecution, but Jesus promised to be with us always.

5. Mark 6:2-6

Underline what Jesus told them.

> *The next Sabbath he went to the synagogue to teach, and the people were astonished at his wisdom and his miracles because he was just a local man like themselves. "He's no better than we are," they said. "He's just a carpenter, Mary's boy, and a brother of James and Joseph, Judas and Simon. And his sisters live right here among us." And they were offended! Then Jesus told them, "A prophet is honored everywhere except in his hometown and among his relatives and by his*

own family." And because of their unbelief he couldn't do any mighty miracles among them except to place his hands on a few sick people and heal them. And he could hardly accept the fact that they wouldn't believe in him (TLB).

What did Jesus say about our relatives and family?

NUGGET: Often, because our family members are so personally acquainted with us, they have a hard time respecting or responding to us and our new life in Christ. It can be somewhat awkward. After all, they know our flaws and human weaknesses. They wonder, *Who do you think you are?* **It's easy for our family to feel like we are judging them, coming across in a self-righteous or holier-than-thou way, which of course is not our intent. Jesus was perfect, yet He was rejected by his own family and friends.**

At times, even our own family members will reject us because of our faith in Jesus Christ. Perhaps you have experienced this very thing. Jesus had some very strong words in Matthew 10:33-39, *"But everyone who denies me here on earth, I will also deny before my Father in heaven. Don't imagine that I came to bring peace to the earth! I came not to bring peace, but a sword. I have come to set a man against his father, a daughter against her mother, and a daughter-in-law against her mother-in-law. Your enemies will be right in your own household!'*

*If you love your father or mother more than you love me, you are not worthy of being mine; or if you love your son or daughter more than me, you are not worthy of being mine. If you refuse to take up your cross and follow me, you are not worthy of being mine. If you cling to your life, you will lose it; but if you give up your life for me, you will find it (NLT).*It's a sad reality that sometimes your enemies will be right in your own household. Make a decision that when this type of rejection comes your way, you will choose to follow Jesus with your whole heart in the midst of the rejection, pain and heartbreak you may feel.

6. Psalm 68:6

Underline the word "solitary."

God sets the solitary in families (NKJV).

What does God do for the solitary?

NUGGET: This passage tells us that God sets the lonely or homeless in families, but I like to look at this passage in another way. When it says that "God sets the solitary in families," could it mean that if you are the first one to be born-again or saved in your family, God will set you as an example and witness to the rest of your family? Does God set the solitary Christian in a family to be a light and beacon for Christ? Being the first person in your family to become a Christ follower is a wonderful and challenging position to be in. It's wonderful to come into a personal relationship with Jesus and if you are the first one in your family to do so, you are blazing a trail for the rest of your family. You have been given the honor, privilege, responsibility and challenge of being a witness for Christ, and as you are led by the Spirit, the Lord will use you to lead the rest of your family to Christ.

7. Proverbs 18:24

Underline the words "closer than a brother."

But there is a friend who sticks closer than a brother (NKJV).

If your family rejects you, who will stick by you even closer than your brother?

Persecution will come, but remember to rejoice and be glad knowing that Jesus will never leave you nor forsake you!

Scriptures to Meditate On

Yes, and all who desire to live godly in Christ Jesus
will suffer persecution.

2 Timothy 3:12, NKJV

But I say to you, love your enemies, bless those who curse you,
do good to those who hate you, and pray for those
who spitefully use you and persecute you.

Matthew 5:44, NKJV

Group Discussion

1. Describe any situations you've faced where your faith in Jesus Christ has cost you and caused you to be rejected or overlooked.

2. Describe any situations where you didn't use wisdom and faced persecution or rejection for your faith that was not necessary. In other words, sometimes we don't use wisdom and good judgment so we bring a certain degree of persecution upon ourselves that is not necessary. Have you ever done that? If so, describe this experience.

3. Describe the way you've handled being persecuted by your family or close friends.

Notes

Notes

Notes

Notes

Notes

Notes

Notes

Notes

ABOUT THE AUTHOR
Beth Jones

Beth Jones and her husband Jeff are the founders and senior pastors of Valley Family Church in Kalamazoo, Michigan, planted in 1991 and named by Outreach magazine as one of the fastest growing churches in America in 2009 and 2010. They also lead Jeff and Beth Jones Ministries, an organization dedicated to helping people *get the basics*. Beth and Jeff have four children who are all involved in leadership and ministry.

Beth grew up in Lansing, Michigan, and was raised as a Catholic. At the end of her freshman year in college, she came into a personal relationship with Christ through the testimony of her roommate. It was there, at age 19, that she realized God's plan for her to preach and teach the gospel through writing and speaking. She has been following that call ever since.

Beth is the author of 20 books, including the popular *Getting a Grip on the Basics* series, which is being used by thousands of churches in America and has been translated into over a dozen foreign languages and used around the world. She also writes *The Basics Daily Devo*, a free daily edevotional for thousands of subscribers.

The heart of Beth's message is simple: *"I exist to help people get the basics!"* Through her practical, down-to-earth teaching, she inspires people to enjoy an authentic relationship with Jesus, to take Him at His Word, and to reach their greatest God-given potential!

Beth attended Boston University in Boston, Massachusetts and received her ministry training at Rhema Bible Training Center in Tulsa, Oklahoma.

For more spiritual growth resources or to connect with Beth, please visit:

www.valleyfamilychurch.org

www.jeffandbethjones.com

www.facebook.com/jeffandbethjones

www.twitter.com/bethjones

www.instagram.com/bethjones

PRAYER OF SALVATION

God loves you—no matter who you are, no matter what your past. God loves you so much that He gave His one and only begotten Son for you. The Bible tells us that "...whoever believes in Him shall not perish but have eternal life" (John 3:16 NIV). Jesus laid down His life and rose again so that we could spend eternity with Him in heaven and experience His absolute best on earth. If you would like to receive Jesus into your life, say the following prayer out loud and mean it from your heart.

Heavenly Father, I come to You admitting that I am a sinner. Right now, I choose to turn away from sin, and I ask You to cleanse me of all unrighteousness. I believe that Your Son, Jesus, died on the cross to take away my sins. I also believe that He rose again from the dead so that I might be forgiven of my sins and made righteous through faith in Him. I call upon the name of Jesus Christ to be the Savior and Lord of my life. Jesus, I choose to follow You and ask that You fill me with the power of the Holy Spirit. I declare that right now I am a child of God. I am free from sin and full of the righteousness of God. I am saved in Jesus' name. Amen.

If you prayed this prayer to receive Jesus Christ as your Savior for the first time, please contact us on the Web at **www.harrisonhouse.com** to receive a free book.

The Harrison House Vision

Proclaiming the truth and the power

Of the Gospel of Jesus Christ

With excellence;

Challenging Christians to

Live victoriously,

Grow spiritually,

Know God intimately.